Age 101
and
Still Having Fun!

A memoir about my Mom, a strong, independent, and unconventional Centenarian who reached the ripe old age of 102 ½

by
Anne Dobkin

Copyright © 2015 by Anne Dobkin

All rights reserved

No part of this book may be reproduced in whole or in part in any form by an electronic or mechanical means without permission in writing by the copyright owner.

Photos included in this book are family photographs. Cover design is a picture of my mother on her 101st birthday

ISBN-13: 978-1508959779

ALL RIGHTS RESERVED

DISCLAIMER

The information given in this book is not meant to be medical advice. No action or inaction should be taken solely on the contents of this information. Before changing your lifestyle or diet, you should consult appropriate health professionals on any matter that involves your health and well- being. The author of this book does not give medical advice or prescribe the use of any technique as a form of treatment for physical medical or emotional problems without the advice of a physician, either directly or indirectly. The intent of the author is only to offer information that her mother used to be happy and healthy throughout her later years of life and to help you to attain your quest for physical, spiritual and emotional well being.

There is nothing in this book that will guarantee a person will live to 100+. But if you are determined to accomplish this feat, it will require you to do your research on the subject matter and change your way of life accordingly. Living a long life comprises many components: your lifestyle, health, family longevity gene pool and just plain good luck!

To my children, Eric and Amanda and my grandchildren, Andrew, Sienna, Allyson, and twins Ryan and Ethan. May they follow my mother's happy and healthy way of life and inherit her longevity genes.

Table of Contents

PREFACE i
ACKNOWLEDGMENTS iii

PART ONE
MOM'S LIFE STORY IN HER OWN WORDS

TURN OF THE CENTURY 1
TRAGEDIES STRIKE 15
CALIFORNIA 23
LUCKY THE HORSE 27
BEVERLY HILLS 31
DRASTIC CHANGES 35
PICKING UP THE PIECES 43
A NEW LIFE EVOLVES 49
A MID-LIFE MOTHER 53
HOLISTIC HEALING 59
THE TEENAGE YEARS 63

PART TWO
MY MOTHER LIKE NO OTHER

MY LIFE WITH MOM 71
SKIMPING AND SAVINGS 73
KEEPING ACTIVE 75
A SPECIAL BOND 79
THE MOVE TO FLORIDA 85
SURVIVING HEALTH ISSUES 89
MOM'S 100th BIRTHDAY PARTY 93
 "OVER THE MOUNTAIN AND READY TO ROLL!" 95
A LETTER FROM YOUR DAUGHTER PAT 97
ASSISTED LIVING FACILITY 103

PART THREE
SECRETS TO A LONG LIFE

- YOU ARE WHAT YOU EAT 111
- YOU ARE WHAT YOU THINK 119
- THE SECRETS TO LONGEVITY 123
- A SUMMARY OF MOM'S LONGEVITY SECRETS 127
- MOM'S TEACHERS 131
- THE SCIENCE OF LONGEVITY 135
- TELOMERES 137
- EPILOGUE 139
- ABOUT THE AUTHOR 141

PREFACE

HOW DOES ONE LIVE TO 100+ AND STILL HAVE FUN!

If my mother could do it there is no reason why anyone can't strive for a long, happy and healthy life. Throughout this book you will learn how my amazing mother reached the ripe old age of 102 ½, and it entails a lot more than just good genes and a lot of luck. She lived through traumatic and life-altering experiences, but with great personal strength, stamina and healthy eating habits, she was able to reach her life long goal of living to 100+ years of age.

Why would I write this book about Mom's long life? What is so unusual and interesting about her that inspired me to tell her story? How was she so different from other mom's that I knew growing up? What did she do at the assisted living facility to still have fun at age 101 and enjoy life? You will find the answers and more as you read her biography. With good luck, long lived gene pool, a change in lifestyle, healthy eating habits, and strong lungs, you might also be given the honor of blowing out all 100 candles on your very special birthday!

One year before her passing, Mom was active and lucid, so I felt that it was time to interview her and record her vital information from her birth to her 101st birthday. I promised her that one day I would write and publish her memoirs and I am thankful that I gathered all her information before her passing. It is not only a great accomplishment to write this book but it is an honor to tell her story to not only interested seniors but to the younger generation as well.

As a child I observed my mother's unconventional way of life, her strange eating habits, her exercise routines and her happy demeanor. I didn't realize at the time that she was not only doing this regiment to keep herself fit and healthy but she was also raising me to be that way as well.

Her daily routines kept her healthy and strong both in body and mind until her last day of life. She was very intelligent, headstrong, feisty and never allowed anyone to take advantage of her. She forged ahead through adversity with a will of iron. She was in charge of her finances, solved her own problems and always had a laugh a day. She was way ahead of her time some 60+ year ago.

I hope you enjoy reading this book and that it will give you the determination and incentive to reach 100+ years of age and still have fun!

ACKNOWLEDGMENTS

Moving to The Villages, Florida has given me the opportunity to learn the different styles of writing and book publishing through the many classes and writing clubs available to the residents of this amazing community. I thank The Villages Recreation Department for providing these venues.

After joining the Abraham-Hicks, Law of Attraction group, I met Nancy Hellekson, the facilitator of this life changing, positive thought, and social group. I am so appreciative for all her educated knowledge she gave me on how to write a manuscript and what steps I had to learn to get self-published on CreateSpace, Amazon's book section. It has been a long, interesting and sometimes frustrating journey getting Mom's book finally published. I thank you so very much for your patience, expertise with self-publishing and knowledge of computers to finally accomplish this task.

PART ONE

Mom's Life Story in Her Own Words

"When life gives you lemons, make lemonade."

CHAPTER 1

TURN OF THE CENTURY

It was a beautiful spring day in South Florida. The date was April 16, 2003 and it was Mom's 101st birthday! She was very excited about her special birthday party at the assisted living facility and wanted me to arrive early. Mom's room was on the first floor by the community area so that she could have easy access to all the activities.

I knocked on the door and it immediately swung open. Her striking aqua blue eyes grew wide as she flashed a big grin. She was very spry and looked much younger than her 101 years!

"Happy Birthday, Mom!" I exclaimed.

"Come in," she said. "I am so happy you made it early so we can spend some time together before my party."

I gave her a big hug and a kiss on her soft cheek.

"How does it feel to have just turned the big 101st year of your long life?"

She smiled and with her usual belly laugh she replied, "The same as yesterday do I look any older?"

"No Mom, you are young in my eyes and still very agile."

"Thank you my darling, now if only my old limbs continue to keep me going, I'll be happy!"

"Mom, it's such a beautiful day, why don't we spend some time sitting in the garden and do some reminiscing about your life."

"That is exactly why I wanted you to come over early. It will be my last wish if you would write a book not only for our family history, but for the general public as well."

"Mom, I will do my best to portray how you lived your long life and reached your final goal as a Centenarian."

As we left her room she proceeded to push her walker down the long hall, continually speaking to me as we strolled outside. She seemed to stop several times to catch her breath.

"Anyone can strive to live a long, happy and healthy life to 100 plus years of age," she said. "They just have to have good luck, good family genes and a burning desire to blow out all those candles! As you know, I have lived a very unconventional life and I did it my way with my many longevity secrets!"

"Mom, you were way ahead of your time. Most people fifty years ago didn't follow the regiments that you and your mother set for yourselves."

"You are correct. Our goal was to stay healthy and happy, striving to reach the big 100th year. Unfortunately, my mother only reached 83 years of age because she had a bad heart valve."

I held the door open for her as she pushed her walker out into the lovely garden. We sat down at a table underneath a large oak tree, surrounded by beautiful spring flowers and the sweet smell of the honeysuckle bushes. I removed a pen and a blank notebook from my bag and began to put her words on paper as she dictated her life story in great detail. She took a deep breath, clearing her throat and began speaking in a determined, but slightly soft voice.

"I was born on April 16, 1902, in Gallion, Alabama, a suburb of Demopolis. My given name is Minnie Laura Stein, and I was later known as 'Billie,' a nickname given to me by a boyfriend. I am the second child in a family of five, and I had three brothers, Sol, Bley, and Alex. My younger sister Joan is still going strong and will be ninety-two on her next birthday. (Joan died soon after Mom's birthday) Alex and Bley died of heart attacks when they were in their fifty's. Sol had cancer and died in his eighty's."

My mother, M Margaret Bley, aka Mema, was born in Tremessen, Germany and came to the United States when she was a teenager,

Her family established roots in Selma, Alabama where she met her husband,

Mom's Family 1906
Front: Mom, Bley, Alex
Back: Sol, Margaret (Mema), Emmanuel

Emmanuel Stein. When my mother turned nineteen years of age they were married. My extended family was quite large. My mother came from a family of nine children and my father from a family of thirteen children."

"Wow!" I exclaimed. "It must have been quite crowded on holidays!"

"Not too bad. We made room for those who wanted to celebrate whatever holiday or birthday that came about. We had some of the family living close by but most lived in other states."

Thanksgiving at Mom's home
1912

"My father had a dry goods store and supported the family on $40 a month. My mother stayed at home to oversee the household chores. We had enough money to hire a nanny to help care for the children as well as a laundress and a cook. The laundress would pick up the dirty clothes, wash them by hand at her home and then carry them back in a basket on her head! The cook would help my mother make delicious homemade meals every night over a wood stove. I remember how cheap the help was. They were each paid just $3.00 per week."

"Our children and grandchildren have no idea what it was like 100 years ago," I said. "They go to the market for food that is already prepared, have an electric washer and dryer to clean their clothes and cook prepared food in a microwave oven. How life has changed!"

"Yes, that is true," she replied. "We did not know any different. Families were closer since everyone had to pitch in and help. We didn't have a computer, television or radio so we had to amuse ourselves with stories, cards and games. It was fun growing up with my brothers and sister being just a few years apart in age."

"My mother whistled and sang as she made the children's clothes on a foot peddled sewing machine," she said. "She could also knit, crochet, and embroider beautiful clothes, sheets and tablecloths. She also made the bedding by hand and stuffed the down and feathers from a goose, into her homemade quilts and pillows."

"Mom, I remember when I was young and you brought out her handmade items from an old trunk you kept in the garage."

"When I moved to the assisted living, it was very hard to make a decision to part with such beautiful, handmade items," she remarked sadly.

"I am so sorry, Mom. Those handmade items must have brought back fond memories of your mother."

"Yes, they did," she said softly.

"So, tell me more about your life growing up in the early 1900's."

"There were no electric lights, the street lamps were hand lit and my family could only see at night by oil lamps. To keep warm our home was heated by coal and a fireplace. We used wood to heat the stove we cooked on.

Most families in the neighborhood did not have an indoor toilet and used an outhouse. My family was better off than most because we had a bathroom inside the home."

"Mom, I can't begin to understand what life was like because today we take for granted flipping a switch for lights, flushing indoor toilets and turning on the air or heat by a control on the wall."

"It was how everyone lived," she said. We did the best we could to survive."

"How did you keep your food cold and free from spoiling?"

"We didn't have refrigeration. A 50 lb. block of ice was delivered to our house each week and it was put into an icebox."

"Did you have a car?"

"Not until much later in the 1920's. We kept a horse in a barn and hitched him up to a buggy when we wanted to get around town."

"What else was different about your life?"

"Our food was fresh and home grown. We kept a cow in the backyard for raw milk. We also raised chickens to eat on special occasions as well as fresh eggs every day."

Friend's and family at Mom's home
1920

"You were fortunate that all your food was healthy, organic and home cooked," I said. "It seems that today people are now striving to return to growing their own food."

"Every family in my town lived a simple life, she said. "We did not have any supermarkets. Everything today is either processed or frozen and that is not food, as I will explain later!"

"Tell me about the styles of clothing you wore."

"We had cinched waists and bustles and no woman dared to show her ankles in public so the clothes were long. Hats and gloves were worn for dress up affairs. Bathing suits covered us to the knees and stockings were worn to hide our legs."

"It must have taken you a long time to get dressed," I remarked.

"Yes, it sure did!" she replied with a chuckle. "The bustles were a pain to do as they had to be cinched tight to show off a small waist. I'm glad they don't have those outfits today. Now, the women want to show off everything! How times have changed in the fashion world!"

"What did you do for fun?"

"My siblings and I amused ourselves by playing with toys made of wood and dolls that were made of cloth. There were ball games during the day and in the evening the family would enjoy playing cards or telling stories. I loved to throw coins into the backyard water well and watch them sink."

"When I was just three years old my older brother Sol and I were playing in the backyard by the well and as I was throwing pennies into it I leaned over too far. Thank goodness my mother was observing us from the kitchen window. She dashed outside and caught me just before I fell into the deep, dark well!"

"Wow! I exclaimed. "You were lucky your mother was looking out the window!"

"Lucky indeed," she replied.

"So, tell me about your school days."

"I really loved going to school. There were only ten classmates in the little red school house. We enjoyed playing hopscotch, jump rope and jacks and my favorite subject was spelling. I had a burning desire to be the best, and I won all the spelling bees!"

Mom became quiet and somewhat agitated before she continued.

"What are you thinking?" I asked. "You seem upset about something".

Mom's eyes looked off into the distance as she shook her head.

"When I was ten year's old there was a terrible tragedy. I remember reading the headlines in the local paper, *'THE TITANIC SINKS, HUNDREDS OF LIVES LOST'!* My parents told me about the many rich and famous people who had taken the cruise. They couldn't believe that an 'unsinkable ship' could sink to the bottom of the icy, cold ocean floor after hitting a large iceberg! Hundreds of people lost their lives that night. The Titanic sinking was one of the biggest events in history, and most people in that era will never forget that tragic disaster."

"I first became aware of what happened to The Titanic when I watched the movie, *A Night to Remember*, on television," I said. "It was so unbelievable and very sad."

"I am glad I didn't see that movie," she replied. "I would not want to be reminded of that horrible event."

"During that time in history were there any other memorable events that you can recall?" I asked.

"I also remember World War I," she replied. "Many soldiers came through my town on the train. One night at a local dance, I met a young man who liked me and it turned into a short, summer romance. He continued to write to me but when he went to war the letters stopped. I was heartbroken as I never knew what happened to my young, soldier boy!"

"I am so sorry to hear that, Mom. It must have been so sad to have lost your first love."

"Yes it was," she said sadly. "But I kept going out with my friends so I could forget about him."

CHAPTER 2

TRAGEDIES STRIKE

Mom's expression was grim and I thought it was about her boyfriend. But, it was regarding another tragic turn of events that was life changing for her.

"What is on your mind?" I asked.

"This is hard to talk about but it is an important part of my young life," she replied.

"I grew up in a happy, loving family atmosphere but when I was twelve years old, a very horrible incident turned my idyllic life upside down!"

"What incident was that?"

My father was having serious financial troubles," she said sadly. "He had a wheat business and the weasels ate all his crops and he couldn't see a way out of saving his dry goods store. My mother was under a lot of stress over this situation so she went to visit nearby relatives and I was left to tend to my siblings."

The family's dry goods store
1914

"I was caring for my baby sister Joan, when I heard a loud pop! I grabbed Joan by the hand and ran into the next room to see what the noise was all about. I was mortified when I saw my father dead on the floor from a gunshot to his head, the gun lying beside him!"

"My God, that's horrible!" I exclaimed.

"I had to think fast," she replied as tears filled her eyes. "I gathered up my siblings and put them in the buggy, hooked up the horse, and rode off to where my mother was staying."

"It was heart wrenching for my family. We were all in shock for many months after the tragedy happened. But, we picked up the pieces and did the best we could to survive emotionally and financially. My mother had to care and support five children on her own and with my help, she persevered. Not only did I have the responsibilities of tending to my siblings needs, but I also had to do most of the chores around the house because we could no longer afford help."

"I am sure she appreciated your help."

"I had no choice, it was expected of me. But as time went on our life grew more stable."

"What were your teen years like?"

"I went to dances and I had many boyfriends because I was told I was a beautiful girl. I was having a wonderful time when another terrible incident happened."

"What now?", I asked with fear in my gut. "You have gone through so much already in your young life!"

"Yes, I have," she replied. "With all the adversities I lived through I survived them all and they made me very strong!"

"That is so true Mom! "You are a real trouper."

I wondered how much more my mother could endure and if I should continue with her life story at this point. It seemed to be getting her down.

"Mom, would you like to take a break and continue later?"

"No, I am fine," she replied.

"So tell me more, what happened next."

She took a deep breath and continued to speak in a soft tone.

"It was a balmy, summer night. My boyfriend picked me up in his shiny, new Model T Ford, along with a few of our friends.

We were very excited because it was the first time we rode in this new mode of transportation. A crank was in the front that needed to be turned many times until the car started. We drove off with great expectations of having a fun night. While we were laughing and enjoying the evening ride we missed the sign that read, *Danger, Road Closed, Do Not Enter*! Unfortunately, we headed down a dark, dirt road where there was an unmarked ditch. The car went over the side of the hill and rolled several times before stopping. We all were seriously injured and it seemed that we laid there in the wrecked car for hours."

"That was awful!", I exclaimed. "How were you found?"

"Later that night, by the 'Grace of God', there was another lost driver who went down the same road," she anxiously replied. "We heard his car and started screaming for help. He heard our screams and found the horrible accident. He told us he would get help and then drove off to alert the nearest hospital. What seemed like forever, two horse drawn ambulances finally arrived and we were all taken to the hospital."

"You were very lucky he found you in time."

"Yes, that is true! I have always wondered if no one found the accident it might have been the end for all of us. There was no way to alert my family as to what happened or where I could be found."

"When I arrived at the hospital, there was a hospital messenger who notified my family. They were told that I had a large forehead laceration, my femur bone was broken in two places and I had a broken hip! Unfortunately, it was another family situation that they all had to endure."

"How long were you in the hospital?"

"I was in the hospital for three months, flat on my back with my leg in a cast. I had to have 22 stitches on my forehead and 6 stitches under my chin. Since the broken leg didn't heal correctly it left me with a permanent limp and constant pain in my knee for most of my life."

"How did you live with such a handicap?"

"I overcame the leg injury by doing yoga and I walked to exercise my knee so it would not stiffen up. For the knee pain I would take aspirin. I did not use any narcotics because I didn't want to be hooked on pain medications."

CHAPTER 3

CALIFORNIA

"I loved being called a 'southern belle' and going to dances. I enjoyed being independent and I was allowed to travel by train to visit my cousin in Montgomery, Alabama. We were very close and we had fun going to parties and dressing up. But, I had to come back to reality and think about what I was going to do with my life."

"Did you have any ideas about your future?"

"I just went along with what life had planned for me. My family decided that they wanted to move to California to be near relatives so I followed along. I was a little scared but also excited to move to a new state and a new environment."

"I finished high school in Los Angeles and after graduation, attended Sophie Newcomb, the Women's College of Tulane University in New Orleans, Louisiana. Most girls were told that they should go to college to find a husband, become a nurse, teacher or secretary. Very few women, in those days, became doctors, lawyers or other professions."

"So, what did you decide to do?"

"I finished college but I still didn't know what I wanted to do with my life. So, I found a job in a notions store paying $18.00 a week. A year later I felt that the job was not going to get me anywhere and I needed to make more money."

"Did you go to a vocational school?"

"Yes, I went to secretarial school and after graduating I was hired to work in an oil company. I enjoyed being an executive secretary, taking shorthand and typing 100 letters a week. For fun, I entered a contest for perfect typing and won a $10.00 prize"

"Sounds like you were striving to be the best you could be."

"I was determined to support myself and be independent. So, after a few years in the oil company, my brother Sol hired me to work in his furniture manufacturing business. He paid me $30.00 a week."

A smile came over her face.

"Mom, why are you smiling?"

"Because I was almost a movie star!"

"How exciting, so tell me more."

"I was reading *The Los Angeles Times* and came across an ad that got my attention. A Hollywood movie studio was having a beauty contest and was looking for women between the ages of 18 and 25. The winner and runner up would have the opportunity of taking a screen test and possibly becoming a Hollywood actress."

"Did you enter the contest?"

"I thought it would be fun so I sent in my picture not thinking I would even come close to winning. I was in shock when I was not only chosen as a contestant but won runner up out of 100+ other beautiful girls!"

"That is amazing! So what happened after you were chosen?"

"A Hollywood producer offered me a screen test and I had to make a quick decision. After thinking about the possibilities of becoming an actress and being famous, it scared me. I was very shy and didn't know how to be an actress. I had insecurities and I felt at that time I could not handle the Hollywood fame. With deep regret I declined the offer."

"Do you now feel that you made a mistake by not taking that opportunity?"

"I always wondered what I would have become and if I would have been successful. It was such a glamorous life and the money would have been great. But, I do believe that everything works out for the best and I felt I had made the right decision. It would have been too stressful and that lifestyle just wasn't for me. Besides, I might not have had you if I was busy with my Hollywood fame!"

CHAPTER 4

LUCKY THE HORSE

"What was your social life like?"

"It was wonderful. I joined a horseback riding club and once a month looked forward to the full moon ride on my horse named 'Lucky'. I truly enjoyed the night rides as well as the socializing afterward. One moonlit night, 'Lucky' was spooked by something, reared up and threw me over his head and I landed on my back."

"Were you hurt?"

"Thank God, no! I was surprised though, when a young, handsome man quickly jumped off his horse and picked me off the ground. I brushed myself off and thanked him. I introduced myself as Minnie Laura Stein and he introduced himself as David Warschauer, and the rest was history! He was attracted to my beauty and shyness and I was attracted to his handsome face and suave mannerisms."

"That sounds so romantic!" What transpired next?"

"We talked after the ride and continued our conversations the next day. David was visiting his cousins in California but lived in Brooklyn, New York. He was an only child, born into a well-respected, wealthy New York family. He made it clear that he was not going out with anyone special at the time and was smitten with me. It seemed I came into his life at the right moment."

"You are right, Mom, the timing was just perfect to begin your relationship. It was divine intervention."

"That, it was! We fell madly in love and were married after a few months of dating. It was meant to be that 'Lucky' reared up and threw me to the ground. David only had eyes for me and I fell for him in a big way, if you know what I mean!"

"That was very funny Mom. Sounds like you were 'twin flames'!"

Looking puzzled she asked, "Twin what?"

Mom and Dad on their Honeymoon
1927

"You were meant to be together. So what happened next?"

"We went on a three month, European honeymoon and cruised on a luxury ocean liner. We arrived in Paris just in time to see Charles Lindbergh land his plane! I was very excited to watch the event and be part of history in the making. I had never been out of the United States so traveling throughout Europe was a wonderful experience, especially on my honeymoon with the man I loved and adored."

CHAPTER 5

BEVERLY HILLS

"After your honeymoon was over where did you live?"

Mom standing in front of her previous Beverly Hills home 1980

"We bought a five bedroom, five bathroom Mexican style home on Alta Drive in Beverly Hills, California. It had a red tile roof and a front courtyard. We paid $25,000 in the 1920's and sold it 15 years later for

$60,000. In the year 2000, it was appraised at $2,000,000!"

"Wow, what a price jump," I remarked. "I remember when we would drive by the house every so often, so you could reminisce about the 'good old days' in Beverly Hills!"

"I really did love that house. I had a lot of fond memories living there for those 20 years. After we settled into the Beverly Hills home, I found out I was pregnant with your older sister, Gertrude, nicknamed "Trudy". Your other sister Patricia, nicknamed "Pat", was born 18 months later. I had an emergency C-Section giving birth to Pat, caused from a placenta previa, and I almost died due to complications from peritonitis. The doctors had a difficult time stabilizing me and when I finally regained consciousness the doctors told me, never to have another child."

"Mom, you were very lucky to have survived another terrible ordeal!"

"It wasn't my time," she said. "I feel so grateful that I lived to see my beautiful, healthy daughters grow up as well as see all my grandchildren and great grandchildren. My guardian angels were by my side all throughout my life!"

"They sure were." I said. "We always have angels to protect us. So tell me about your life in Beverly Hills."

"Trudy and Pat attended Beverly Hills High School and enjoyed their teen years there. We were surrounded by affluent neighbors, such as Elizabeth Taylor and other movie stars. We had a household of servants to do the laundry, take care of the girls, do the landscaping maintenance, as well as a chauffeur to drive us around town. We also had a Jamaican cook/housekeeper named 'Rose' who was like a second mom and lived with the family for fifteen years."

"Since you had so much free time what did you do all day?"

"David and I played golf and we traveled. When we were home, David spent his leisure time playing his Steinway grand piano and writing music and books."

"I wonder if that is why I have the desire to write. I feel Dad is with me in spirit and he is helping me complete this book. I also have three more books after this one so that should keep him busy!"

"I am sure he will be guiding you. Since it is your first book it will be quite a project."

"I was wondering how you could afford the Beverly Hills home since you and Dad did not work?"

"David had a $3,000 a month trust fund set up by his father to cover all of his expenses for life."

"It must have been nice to live a luxurious lifestyle and not worry about how the bills were going to be paid!"

"Yes, I married well but also adored your father for richer or poorer!"

CHAPTER 6

DRASTIC CHANGES

"What was it like after the stock market crashed in 1929 and then later, the start of World War II?"

"In 1929 David's father had a seat on the New York stock exchange. He was heavily invested in the market with the money he made in his successful, New York hat business. Unfortunately, he lost three million dollars overnight, had a heart attack and died. David's mother followed, dying a few months later. David was heartbroken and grew closer to the only family he had, his wife and two children. Losing both parents in a matter of a few months was more than he could take."

"How sad," I said.

"Yes, it was very sad, but David knew he had to move on and keep busy. Our life in Beverly Hills was ideal, to say the least. We were all happy until Pearl Harbor was bombed and we had to make some big decisions."

"That sounds frightening!" I exclaimed.

"It was very concerning. David grew very anxious and distraught because he was afraid that California would be next. After deep thought about the dire circumstances, he convinced me to sell the Beverly Hills home and move to New York. Reluctantly, I gave in. I was sad to leave a home I had lived in for so many years and would miss my friends and relatives. We sold our home within a month and moved 3,000 miles away to Lake Placid, New York. We rented a large house overlooking Lake Placid. It was a beautiful setting and very relaxing."

"That was quite a change for you and the family."

"Yes, it was exhausting to move but we managed it all. Trudy and Pat were not happy about leaving their home, school and friends but it didn't take them long to get acclimated. They quickly made new friends and seemed to like the small town atmosphere. We spent the summer enjoying waterskiing on the lake in our new ski boat as well partaking in snow skiing during the long, cold winter."

"Sounds like you made the right decision to move."

"Yes, we made the right decision and we finally were enjoying life after the long trip to Lake Placid. We settled into our new home and all was going well until I started to feel sick. I was gaining weight, felt nauseous and at 43 years old I thought I was going through early menopause symptoms. I went to see the family doctor, who examined me and ran some tests. A week went by when the doctor called with some shocking news. He told me I was pregnant!"

"What a surprise! I guess it was meant for me to be here to write a book about your long life!"

"It was meant to be and it all worked out in the divine plan of life. But at the time, I didn't know if I should have jumped for joy or cry in fear! What would I do with a baby in midlife, especially at a time when my daughters were ages 15 and 17 and almost grown?"

"You were in quite a predicament. I don't know what I would have done."

"I knew that having another baby at my age could be life threatening! It was a very difficult decision your Dad and I had to make! Not only did I worry about my health and possibly not making it through the delivery, but I had another dilemma to ponder."

"So, what was that?"

"It was World War II and if I decided to have an abortion it was going to be difficult finding a competent doctor. After much contemplation, and talking it over with your Dad, he felt my life was more important. So we searched around and finally found a doctor willing to perform the abortion."

"I am lost for words! This sounds like it was a serious decision to make!"

"Yes, it was! But it was either my life that was at stake or losing both of us during the delivery. So your Dad and I made the decision to go ahead with the abortion.

"So what happened next?"

"We arrived at an old, dingy office on a back street. The doctor came out of the back room smelling of alcohol. We had a short conversation with him and then he proceeded to show David his special gun collection. We both became very uneasy and we were having second thoughts about going through with the procedure. At that point, David grabbed my arm and we ran out of the office. His mind was made up, I was going through with the pregnancy and he felt that it was better to take a chance with professional obstetricians then to lose my life in a botched abortion!"

"Oh my God!" I exclaimed. "I just realized it would have been only a matter of minutes when I could have been gone. I guess everything happens for a reason and I am grateful that you and Dad made that important decision not to go through with the abortion."

Mom held my hand and stared at me with her tired blue eyes.

"My darling daughter, it was God's plan that you are here with me today. I could not have lived this long without you as you kept me young. You also took charge of my life when I could no longer care for myself in my home and I am so grateful to have had you in my life".

Tears came to my eyes and she gave me a tissue to wipe them dry.

"It took me some time to accept the pregnancy but after a period of time it all worked out and my life situation turned out for the best! I finally looked forward to having a baby again and my relationship with your Dad was the best it had been in a long time. He was so looking forward to having a new baby in the house. But the news of the pregnancy was a shock to Trudy and Pat since they were teenagers and they had a hard time accepting the fact that their mother was pregnant at 43 years old."

"I can understand their feelings," I said. "Most kids their age think their parents no longer have sex in mid-life."

Mom was blushing as she smiled at me.

Trudy, Pat, Mom, Anne, Dad and Peter
1946

"We surprised them! As time went on into my pregnancy everyone looked forward to your arrival. I had good care and confidence in my doctors. I was scheduled for another C-section on April 3rd at Saranac Hospital in Lake Placid. That morning, your Dad felt compelled to be close to God so he went up to the nearby mountain and he prayed and meditated. The C-section went well without any complications and you were born that morning, healthy and weighed six pounds, five ounces. Your Dad was elated that you and I were doing just fine and everything went well!"

"Thank God!" I exclaimed. "I am so happy that everything turned out in a positive way."

"Yes, it all turned out just fine. We brought you home and I had a full-time baby nurse for a few months so everyone could get a rest. Our life had changed in a big way."

CHAPTER 7

PICKING UP THE PIECES

"How long did you live in Lake Placid?"

Mom, Dad and me on The Atlantic City Boardwalk
1947

"We lived another year in Lake Placid and then spent some time in Atlantic City, New Jersey. We were staying in a hotel along the boardwalk, enjoying the long walks we took with you in your carriage and riding in a push cart. Christmas had just passed when Trudy decided to visit a friend and left on the train in a blinding snowstorm. Pat stayed behind with us in Atlantic City."

Mom grew quiet for a minute. She looked as though she was in deep thought.

"What is on your mind, Mom?"

"This is difficult to talk about," she replied.

"Take your time. Would you like a few minute break?"

"No, I am ok," she said softly.

She shook her head and took a deep breath, cleared her throat and proceeded to speak slowly.

"It was a cold winter morning when David decided he needed to get out of the hotel and take a walk alone. When he returned to the hotel room, about an hour later, he told me he didn't feel well and went to lie down on the bed."

She again breathed a deep sigh and continued speaking in a cracking voice, as the tears rolled down her face.

"You don't have to talk about this if it is getting you too upset," I said.

"It is important to have you write this down," she replied. "Don't worry, I'll get through it."

She wiped her eyes and blew her nose with a tissue. She began speaking in a soft voice.

"Your Dad was having trouble breathing and I decided to call the house doctor. But when the doctor arrived it was too late. He had passed away of a heart attack!"

She wiped away more tears from her tired, blue eyes.

"What a terrible shock you must have gone through!" I exclaimed. "I am so sorry, Mom. It must have been devastating for everyone."

She was sobbing and I put my arms around her and held her tight. We both had a good cry for a few minutes. She took another deep breath and continued to talk.

"Yes. it was overwhelming. I did not know what to do at that time as we were vacationing in Atlantic City. Trudy was away visiting her friend, you were just one and a half years old, playing with your bunny toy in your crib and Pat was crying uncontrollably. I had to stay strong as I felt so alone. In the blink of an eye I had suddenly lost the man I adored and had been married to for almost 20 years!"

She took another deep sigh.

"David's $3,000 a month income was going to be terminated at his demise and I didn't know if there was going to be any money for me or my girls. I had you to bring up and everything was so overwhelming, my mind was in a fog!"

I held her hand as she continued to speak.

"So many questions filled my mind. How was I going to bring up a baby alone? Where were we going to live? What now? It all seemed so surreal. I fell into a deep, dark void."

"Mom, you had a lot to contend with. How did you manage to get your wits about you?"

"My mother was in California and I had no one around for any moral support", she said. "I had to snap out of this horrible situation and pull myself out of the depression I was in. I was the only family member to make the funeral arrangements, pack up the car and start a new life."

"There are times in life where one has a choice to either sink or swim and Mom, you are a swimmer! I am so proud of you!"

"I had no other choices. After the funeral and burial in Brooklyn, New York, I decided to move to Los Angeles, California to be near my family. I had the furniture shipped and I drove across the country with just you and the dog. Trudy and Pat were off to college. I had very little income, no place to live, a toddler, two young adults and a dog to take care of!"

"I don't know if I could have been so brave to uproot the family and drive alone across the country," I said.

"You do what you feel is the best decision and being near my family was important."

CHAPTER 8

A NEW LIFE EVOLVES

Mom was now a single mother, alone and on her way to California to start a new life.

"How did you survive?"

"I was very fortunate. In the will your Dad left me $400 a month in annuities to live on. Your grandfather also provided for you girls with the rest of the estate divided up and given to the three of you when you turned 21 years of age. It all worked out and when I arrived in California I found an apartment in downtown Los Angeles."

"Did you move close by your family?"

"Yes, I did. They all lived just a short distance away in Los Angeles. My mother was a great comfort and she gave me much needed encouragement and guidance, as well as being my babysitter at times. The apartment was near a beautiful area called 'Westlake Park' and it had a serene lake with motorboats. I only had myself and you to think about as Trudy and Pat were still in a Georgia college at that time."

"I remember playing on the playground and enjoying the boat rides with you and 'Mema," I said. Life was beginning to get a whole lot better for us."

"It sure was, life was good. I felt I was making the right decisions at that time and I think your Dad was guiding us along the way as well! A year later, I found out that my favorite uncle had passed on. I had another loss to deal with but out of my grief came a big surprise. My uncle had left me $30,000 in his will!"

"You were very lucky to have inherited that money. It came at a perfect time."

"Yes, I was very lucky to have received the perfect amount to buy a home for us to live in. Pat and Trudy were coming back to Los Angeles to find jobs and planned to live with us. It didn't take long before I found a cozy bungalow to buy in Westwood, near my old home site in Beverly Hills. Our new home had three bedrooms and two bathrooms. The backyard had fruit trees galore and was situated in a safe neighborhood. We had finally established roots!"

The Westwood home where Mom lived for 50 years.

CHAPTER 9

A MID-LIFE MOTHER

"Tell me about your life as a single Mom and what it was like bringing me up?"

"At middle age it was not easy, you really kept me on my toes! When you were only three years old I bought the Westwood house. Mema and your sisters helped me move in and while we were unpacking boxes and putting items away, you escaped and went out the door to look around the neighborhood. In a panic, we realized you were missing. After searching the area for a few hours, we found you sitting by a pond in a neighbor's yard. You were scolded and taken back home."

"I was a handful, wasn't I?"

"You sure were!" she replied, with a belly laugh. "I was very busy getting the house in order and I gave your sisters the responsibility of watching your every move. Of course they were not too happy about that job. They had a busy life of their own and it seemed that they did not want to be bothered."

"I heard all about it from their perspective," I said. "What other situations did I cause you to stress out?"

Mom had a big grin on her face.

"When it was time for potty training I would have to tie you to the toilet seat with a rope around your waist and then knot it tightly. It didn't work, and within a short time you figured out how to undo each and every knot and get off the toilet seat!"

"That is really funny," I said. "I am still that way today! If I have a problem, I always try and solve it!"

"That is a good trait," Mom replied.

"Do you remember getting me my first dog?"

"Oh yes, that was a big decision. When you were five years old you begged me to get you a dog. But, I felt a dog would require too much care and responsibility for your age and

I was not interested in feeding or walking a dog."

"But you finally gave in, didn't you Mom?"

"Yes, reluctantly I did."

"I remember when we were visiting Aunt Adele, and someone gave her an eight-week old dachshund puppy," I said. "I asked you if I could have him because she did not want the dog. When you said 'yes', I jumped for joy!"

"Looking back, I realized it was the best decision for you to have a dog to play with. It also taught you how to care for him and be responsible."

"Speaking of dogs Mom, do you remember Mother's Day at Aunt Adele's house when I got lost in the Hollywood Hills?"

"Do I remember! That is the day I will never forget. Her home was isolated and nestled away in the Hollywood Hills and you took off with her dog and went for a hike. When we realized you were nowhere to be found we all went looking for you. By dusk we gave up and called the police."

"I remember I was very scared", I said. "The dog ran away, left me alone in the woods and I didn't know how to get back to Aunt Adele's house. I knew I was lost so I sat down by a stream and cried. I was praying that you would find me before it got dark!"

"Thankfully, the police finally found you! I was elated that you were safe but on the other hand, I was very upset with you because you ran away again!"

"I did learn a big lesson", I replied.

"It was about time! I could never understand why you liked to just disappear."

"I guess I felt free, thinking nothing bad could ever happen to me."

While growing up, Mom needed time away from me and a life of her own. She was out quite often, going to her dancing lessons, exercise classes, luncheons, and whatever else she did to keep busy. But as I grew older, I realized she did the best she could as a mid-life, single mother.

When she was home, she managed to take me to and from school, piano lessons, dance lessons, swimming, ice skating and more. Even though she was the oldest mother in my school, as well as a Girl Scout leader, she had the drive and determination to prove to herself to take on the job with vim and vigor! Some of my friends made hurtful comments about Mom being too old, but I ignored them and felt proud of her and all of her accomplishments

CHAPTER 10

HOLISTIC HEALING

When I was eight year's old there were some concerns that crossed my mind at times. I always feared that if Mom died or became sick who would take care of me. Low and behold the worst of my fears came to fruition.

"Mom, do you remember the time you were sick and I called Mema to come over and take care of us?"

"I do remember. It was a very scary time!"

"What happened to you that caused you to go from a very vibrant person to one that could hardly get out of bed?" I asked.

"I did not know what was wrong with me she replied. I was very weak from loss of blood and I thought it was just menopause symptoms."

"You really got me very concerned when you had to hold onto the wall to walk!"

"I thank you for being so concerned my dear, I thought I could handle everything. I now realize I was not rational at that time. I am glad you were smart enough to pick up the phone and call Mema."

"I was so relieved when she was there to help take care of us," I said. "She was a wonderful German cook and I was happy that she fed you nourishing food as well as making sure you took your vitamins and herbs to get you back to health."

"She was a Godsend," she said. "I had no one else to help me. My mother sensed something was wrong, that it could be life threatening and told me it was time to see a doctor. I agreed and made an appointment. The doctor told me I had large, uterine fibroids and that he wanted to perform a hysterectomy to stop the bleeding. I did not want surgery and elected to heal myself".

"Mom, you were taking on quite a risk. But, with your strong will to bypass any medical procedures and medicines, you miraculously healed yourself! You have a strong belief in God and the natural, holistic way of healing and it always seemed to work for you!"

"Yes, you could say that. But my way is not what most people would try. Not everyone believes they can heal themselves through positive thinking, fresh whole foods, natural medicines, a strong will, and trust in a higher power. When I found out my problems were from bleeding fibroids, I took action. Every day I would lie on my slant board, with my feet higher than my head, and an ice pack on my pelvis. The bleeding soon stopped and I was slowly getting back to my routine."

"It really was a miracle Mom, when after just a few weeks you completely recovered without an operation."

CHAPTER 11

THE TEENAGE YEARS

As a mid-life mother, Mom anxiously lived through my teenage years. It was a different time when she was raising my sisters, some 30 plus years ago.

"What was it like raising a teenager again?"

"Very trying. You were going through the hippy, free love era and I had a hard time with you breaking my house rules."

"That's funny, Mom. Being a teenager, I had a lot of friends and activities such as going to the beach, dances, movies and hanging out. Even though I was fearless and strong willed, I tried not to upset you too much."

"I must say, you turned out ok!"

"Remember my best friend Helen, the hot blond with a great figure who allured all the boys around us?"

"Do I remember Helen!" she exclaimed. "I was good friends with her mother and we use to compare our concerns. Thank goodness no one got in trouble, if you know what I mean!"

"You really did not have to worry, everything turned out fine. We graduated from high school and she went to The Valley College while I went to UCLA so I could live at home and save money."

"That was a good choice. But after college you decided to get an apartment with a roommate and I missed you being at home. Then you met Rick and moved six hours away to ski with him at Mammoth Mountain, California."

Mom was sad about seeing me leave. It was a big change for her but she was determined to go on with her life and refused to be downhearted and alone.

"You fell in love with Rick and had a beautiful garden wedding. I wished you well and waved goodbye as you left on your honeymoon across the country. You settled in New Jersey where you lived for the next 17 years. I missed you but I realized that life must go on."

Mom's 101 Birthday
April 16th 2003

"Mom, you seem very tired right now, maybe it is time to end your life story."

"Yes, I think it is time to end this conversation. I need to rest up for my big party this afternoon. Did I give you enough information to begin writing my book?"

"You gave me more than enough and I thank you from the bottom of my heart. This will give people an incentive to follow your longevity secrets, have hope when life gets them down and live a healthy, long life as you have done."

"That would make me very happy," she said.

I helped her up from the bench and gave her a big hug. We walked back to her room and with great excitement, she proceeded to get dressed for her party. I felt so blessed to have been able to see Mom celebrate her 101st birthday. She was the star of the show and as always, loved all the attention. She was definitely a party girl!"

FROM 1902 to 2004
Mom experienced the following:

Horse drawn buggy	Ice Box
Oil Lamps	Out House
World War I	World War II
Wood stove for cooking	Coal for heating
First airplane	First Model T Ford Car
1929 Stock Market Crash	Great Depression
Flapper Era	Jitterbug dancing
Lindbergh Kidnapping	Prohibition
Women's Suffrage	Women's Liberation
Paved Roads	Crank Wall Telephones
Radio	Records
Electric Washing Machine	Television
The Beatles	Elvis
Hippy, Free Love	Space Travel
Jet Planes	Sky Scrapers
Computers	Stereo Sound System
CD/DVD players	Cell Phones

PART TWO

"My Mother Like No Other!"

"Live, Love and Laugh Each and Every Day!"

CHAPTER 12

MY LIFE WITH MOM

From my prospective there is so much more to tell about Mom's life then what she had dictated. From the time I could remember, which was about five years old, I was along for quite the ride of my young life right up to her demise at 102 ½!

Mom had many tragedies in her long life but she chose to overcome them and move ahead. Her happy demeanor and positive outlook on life got her to the status of Centenarian. She believed in a belly laugh a day, not only for the mind but to stimulate the organs. She always said, "People who laugh a lot, live longer". Now I know why she had a sense of humor.

Today, at age 69, I am thankful that I learned her *roadmap to life*. She brought me up to follow her unconventional eating habits, holistic health regiments and positive outlook on life. All of which I thought at the time, to be very out of the norm compared to all the other mothers I knew. I now realized that what she did, all made sense. I have put her way of life into practice to enhance my life today.

I live in The Villages, Florida, a retirement community of over 100,000 residents. It is a place where I can partake of all the activities to keep me young and active. There are many holistic and spiritual classes as well as sports and exercise centers to keep me fit and in shape, both mentally and physically. Also, there are many organic food classes as well as a fresh market to buy whole, organic foods from the local farms. I do feel blessed that what I had learned from Mom growing up, I can put into practice here

.

CHAPTER 13

SKIMPING AND SAVINGS

After my Dad passed on, Mom was left a $400 a month annuity. Because she had no financial experience she had to be creative so she could pay her bills and save a little money. She did not have current skills to get a job, so she decided to get her real estate license. She passed the test and was hired. After many months of trying to sell houses she found it to be too time consuming and cut throat, so she quit. How she was able to pay her bills and save money was really amazing.

Mom was a good shopper and was never without clothes or household items. Thrift shops were places she liked to do her treasure hunting. Not only did she buy designer clothes but also bric-a-brac and antique furniture that she would fix up and sell for extra money at her many garage sales. She also would take in foreign UCLA medical students and rent out my previous bedroom and bath for $500 a month to get more income and to have someone in the house at night.

She instilled in me her two favorite sayings: 1. "If you don't have the money you don't buy it" 2. "Never borrow, never lend". There were no credit cards at that time and she had to have the cash to buy whatever she wanted. She didn't believe in being in debt and was very fortunate her house and car were paid for.

CHAPTER 14

KEEPING ACTIVE

Mom was always going somewhere, a homebody she was not! When she was planning to be out at night she would lie on her slant board with slices of cucumber on her eyes to get rid of puffy, dark circles. She would also take a nap to get refreshed and in a few hours she was good to go!

She enjoyed reading the newspaper, and one day came across an ad that said, *"Win a week of Arthur Murray dance lessons."* She was very excited when she entered the contest and won! One week of dancing turned into 10 years of lessons, competition and fun parties. Ballroom dancing was a wonderful outlet for her and she entered into all the dance competitions, sometimes winning first place. If she were alive today, *'Dancing with the Stars'* would have been her favorite TV show and if she lived in The Villages she would be dancing every night somewhere in the town!

Mom's dance picture
1957

Mom was thrifty and bought her long dance gowns at bargain prices in second hand stores. On the night of a competition, she would get her hair done, apply her makeup, and dress in one of her long, flowing gowns. She felt very pretty, loved dancing all night, the exercise, the competitions and the social interaction with other ballroom dancers.

She was a very social person and enjoyed going to fashion shows and luncheons. She belonged to a few women's clubs and read the latest fashion magazines and newspapers. Even though designer outfits were out of her budget, she would still enjoy going to the big department stores in Beverly Hills. Sometimes she was lucky and found a dress or handbag on clearance.

Mom also enjoyed going to the gym. She would swim and do many laps in the pool, until she was in her 90's. She knew quite well that in order to keep limber one must exercise every day.

Bridge was another one of Mom's activities. She was a 'Life Master Player' and spent a lot of time studying the intricate card game. Bridge kept her mind sharp because it is an ongoing learning process. She persevered and won many tournaments with her partner.

When she was 55 years old, she joined a senior citizen recreation center. She spent her time at the center attending lectures, card games, and other daily activities. There were occasional trips to Las Vegas, which she

Keeping Active

referred to as 'lost wages'! The slot machines were her favorite and she was very lucky, hitting a few big jackpots, winning her money back, and then some.

One summer she traveled on a cruise ship to Hawaii. She learned the Hula and enjoyed eating poi and roasted pig! Photography was one of her new hobbies and she bought a manual SLR camera with lenses. She learned how to use the camera and took many beautiful, photographic slides of the islands.

Mom on a cruise ship to Hawaii
1955

CHAPTER 15

A SPECIAL BOND

Mema's 80th Birthday

Mom and Mema were very close and they spent a lot of time together. Mema had a big influence on Mom's demeanor. Being of German ancestry she was also independent, strong-willed and self-directed. Their common interests were in health foods and they had the same health regiments.

Mom and Mema walked the Hollywood Hills together and enjoyed nude sunbaths in secluded places. At that time, they felt the sun was healing and never used sunscreen. Believe it or not, they never had a single skin cancer. They knew that the sun was good for their bones as well as vitamin D absorption.

They were obsessed with not only health foods but unconventional workout routines. They both loved to watch *'Yoga for Health'* and would stand on their heads, do difficult positions and sit in the lotus poses. They felt the breath was very important and would breathe deeply, in through the nose, holding it for five seconds and then exhaling out through the mouth.

They also watched, *Jack La Lane Show* daily, and did their jumping jacks, stretching movements and other routines, along with Jack, to keep limber. I thought they were both loony. I have come to realize that all those regiments were just their quest to be healthy and add years to their lives.

Gilman Hot Springs, California, was a interesting resort where Mom and Mema would vacation and get rejuvenated. It was a big part of their health regiment. They would spend almost the whole day in the spa. It was a wonderful place for them to relax and detox. They would take mud baths, then shower and get wrapped in wool blankets to sweat for an hour. After that routine they would get a salt massage, take another shower, and then go up to the roof of the spa for nude sunbaths. I was so embarrassed when I went to the roof looking for them, but it seemed they were not modest.

Mom, Mema and I would walk down a path which led into a deep, mineral well that smelled like rotten eggs. The mineral water flowed down the sides of the rocks into a small pond. They would scoop the mineral water into pitchers and after filling them would take the pitchers back to their cabins. Throughout their stay, they repeated the trek back and forth to the mineral well to collect and drink more mineral water. I thought this was weird but they felt the water had healing properties that made their immune system stronger.

Mom, Mema and I also spent many summers at Lake Arrowhead, California. It was a beautiful mountain town with a large lake for swimming and boating. Mom and Mema rented a cabin in the woods and we would walk to town and the lake. Mema had asthma and she seemed to think the mountain air helped her condition. It made her breathe harder and helped her lungs to expand. The smell of the fresh pine scented the air and was so exhilarating. We felt being in nature helped us to relax and feel at peace.

Mom and me at Lake Arrowhead
1954

Even today, I long for the mountains and lakes in the summer time. I feel closer to God and nature, which is good for my spiritual health and happiness.

CHAPTER 16

THE MOVE TO FLORIDA

Mom had been very independent as well as self-sufficient in her later years and she didn't need anyone telling her how to run her life. It took a lot to convince her at 95, that she no longer had the capabilities to walk up and down the stairs nor remember to take care of her daily responsibilities. Also, she could no longer see over the wheel of her car. She had a few minor accidents resulting in her insurance company cancelling her policy and the Department of Motor Vehicles voiding her license.

Mom never seriously injured herself in her home. But unfortunately, the inevitable finally did happen. She fell and needed a dozen stitches. She called the doctor and had to be taken to the emergency room. I felt it was time for her to think about moving to Florida and be near me to handle her medial care and financial business. When I mentioned this to her she made it known that, "she never wanted to leave her home and that the men in the white coats would have to carry her out".

Mom was depressed about losing her independence. She still wanted to keep up her daily activities. In order to get here and there, she hired cabs and sometimes got a neighbor to drive her. But relying on the neighbors or a few friends didn't last long. Her life was becoming more difficult and she finally realized that moving to Florida was the best decision for her.

Mom never let anything get her down for long. She was still independent, self-directed and feisty. She hired a realtor and put her home up for sale. She also found a lady to help her clean out closets and pack up boxes, which took them three months to complete.

She had beautiful antiques and hand carved furniture, including a Steinway grand piano, silver serving pieces and gold plated china from England. She was able to sell it all for top dollar. She also collected a lot of stuff after living in her home for almost a half a century and gave it all away to the different charities and thrift shops. Her garage was full of old trunks with clothes and ancient items from the years she lived in Beverly Hills. Even her wedding gown was packed in one of the trunks. She felt very sad when she had to give away her old, musty belongings as they were a big part of her life in Beverly Hills. It was really quite a feat for her to manage to get rid of everything by the day of the closing.

By the time I arrived in California, the house was empty. I was impressed that, at her age, she did such a great job getting her place in order to sell. She had many offers on her house and finally settled on one close to the asking price. After the closing we boarded the plane and flew to Boca Raton, where she lived until her passing.

CHAPTER 17

SURVIVING HEALTH ISSUES

For Mom's 99th birthday, my sister decided to send her a new, three-wheeled walker with a seat. She tried it out and fell over it, breaking her leg. I got the call that Mom was in the hospital and needed surgery right away. She stayed in the hospital for a week and then was sent to a rehab/nursing home for therapy.

She hated being in the rehab/nursing home. Even though the facility was brand new and pleasing to the eye, Mom could not cope with her environment. She begged me every day, "to please take her out of this hell hole"! Most of the patients had dementia or Alzheimer's and were crying or yelling all day. Some sat around the nurse's station tied to their wheelchairs. Others were walking the halls holding teddy bears and crying out for their mother.

Mom worked very hard at her rehab exercises and was released early when she could walk again. All her friends and family were amazed at how fast she recovered. We felt it was her strong determination that got her out of the rehab sooner than later and back to her routine at the ALF.

Mom found a lump in her breast and told me, "at her age she was not going to do anything about it". She did not want any treatments or surgery. Her 100th birthday was coming up and she wanted to be able to celebrate with her family. Also, her granddaughter was getting married in a few months and she was determined to walk down the aisle. Her wishes were respected and no one knew her secret until after the wedding.

After living with the lump for a year, it grew the size of a golf ball, popped out of the skin and was bleeding. The doctor felt it was time to remove it along with the breast. She was not happy about surgery but followed the doctor's orders and decided to have a mastectomy and remove the festering lump. The surgeon told me, "it was cancer but miraculously the cancer never spread". A few lymph nodes had been removed and she had no treatments. She healed fast, was cancer free, and back to the ALF activities in no time!

When Mom was 101 years of age she had congestive heart failure and was admitted to the hospital. She stayed overnight and when I went to visit her she was sitting in a chair watching television. She did not like the hospital food and when she found out that the cost of her room was $200 per night she decided that the hospital was too expensive and checked herself out. She called the ALF van to pick her up immediately and bring her back to the comforts of her living arrangements and daily activities.

CHAPTER 18

MOM'S 100th BIRTHDAY PARTY

Mom and I at her birthday party
April 16, 2002

It was a beautiful day in south Florida and all the relatives arrived from different parts of the United States to celebrate her big birthday. The party was held in a French restaurant near the ALF and Mom was all dressed up in a beautiful, deep blue silk suit. She had her hair and nails done as well as her makeup. She really looked ten years younger than her 100 years. She glowed with excitement and loved being the center of attention. She was disappointed that the restaurant would not allow her to put 100 lighted candles on her cake, so she chose to put a single 100th birthday candle in the middle of the cake surrounded by 12 candles for her 3 children, 7 grandchildren and 2 great grandchildren.. She had many gifts and colorful balloons surrounding her table. It was quite the celebration!

CHAPTER 19

"OVER THE MOUNTAIN AND READY TO ROLL!"

I wrote and read the following poem to Mom at her birthday party:

"One hundred years have passed by and Mom, you are still very spry! You have a mind that is still clear as day, and you know how to always find your way. Nothing ever gets you down, as you are not bound by any person, situation or frisky hound."

"You hardly smoked or ate processed foods nor had much of an interest in a horny dude! You have a few belly laughs now and then, even a few swigs of gin. You are independent, feisty and strong willed as can be, is all this a secret to your longevity?"

"The doctor is amazed by good health at your age." 'How can this be?' says he. 'She must have a special gene, one that is rarely seen. Who in this family carries this trait, or could it be just her fate?'

"To have lived so long and seen so much: two world wars, radio TV and computers as such. How lucky you are to celebrate this special date, you definitely are not ready for the pearly gate?"

"It is wonderful to have your family here, to celebrate your BIG 100th YEAR! Rejoice Mom, and may your birthday be filled with happiness and fun, because the game of life you have already won!"

"So, Mom just remember one thing, whatever you do I will always love you!"

CHAPTER 20

A LETTER FROM YOUR DAUGHTER PAT

Things I remember about Mom, read to her on her 100th birthday:

"You loved to clean out closets, beginning with the store room in our Beverly Hills home. Out would come boxes of yellow newspapers from World War I. Grandfather's pinched nose glasses with the long, black ribbon. A beautiful accordion purchased in Switzerland on your honeymoon. Dad said to the street vendor, 'I'll buy your accordion if you teach me how to play that song'. The vendor immediately taught Dad the song and he bought the accordion."

"There were boxes of stuff in this store room, such as old shoes, old hats, dog leashes, many old pictures of long, gone relatives, old clothes, and your size 10 wedding gown which Trudy and I played dress up in. You *tossed out some junk and kept other items that were put aside until the next time you did your yearly cleaning!"*

"Sixty years ago, this cleaning out and sorting stuff became a cottage industry, better known as 'the yearly garage sale'! You were very good at this, and had the knack to sell things quickly. You even went to garage sales to pick up antiques, old and valuable pieces of china, crystal, vases, furniture, and old, blacken antique silver amid someone else's junk. Then you would fix up everything you bought, to keep for yourself, or resell them at one of your future garage sales, making a big profit!"

"I remember Rose, our cook/housekeeper you hired when you first moved to Beverly Hills. Rose was like a second mom to us and she stayed over 17 years. She was a wonderful cook and would make delicious cakes like, chocolate truffle, graham cracker crust with raspberry filling and cheesecakes."

"I remember the home movies you loved to show us about your honeymoon in Europe.

A Letter From Your Daughter Pat

Also the movies when Trudy and I were babies, growing up in Beverly Hills and having fancy birthday parties with clowns as the entertainment."

"You were a Brownie and Girl Scout leader. Also you were a 'nurse' who would rub our legs with oil every night when we had growing pains. When we came down with a cold or flu you would get out the Vick Vapor Rub and apply it to our chest and use a heat lamp for colds and flu. Rose would bring trays of water, vitamin C pills and fresh, squeezed orange juice to us upstairs. You gave us Milk of Magnesia if we were constipated, yuk! You would take us to Palm Springs to sit in the warm, desert sun to rid me of my bronchitis and Trudy of her hay fever."

"You and dad would love to go to many restaurants in Beverly Hills for special occasions. The average price for dinner was $1.50 per person and half price for children, what a deal!"

"I remember when you and Mema would go to Gilman Hot Springs to rest, relax and to detox the poisons out of your body. At the spa, you and Mema would take mud baths, nude sun baths, get massages and drink smelly mineral water from the mineral spring."

"To be well rounded in the arts you took us to singing, piano and violin lessons as well as art, golf, tennis, archery, horseback riding, drama, swimming, diving, ballet, tap, and ice skating activities."

"When Christmas came it was a big celebration at our house. We always had a tall tree in the living room and then you and dad would burn the tree in the fireplace the day after Christmas. It was fun hearing the burning pine crackle and pop and the pine tree smell was divine!"

"You worked hard for the war effort and knitted navy blue helmets for our boys overseas. You also volunteered at the USO."

A Letter From Your Daughter Pat

"We moved to Lake Placid, New York and you gave birth to our little sister, Annie. You and dad were so happy, while we didn't know what to make of the situation with a crying baby in the house. Our dates wondered whose baby it was and there was a lot of explaining to do!"

"Sadly, dad died suddenly at the age of 47, in a hotel room we were staying at in Atlantic City. You were left a single mom with a baby, 21 pieces of luggage and a dog, and moved everyone to California where you lived for the next 50 years."

"I had some money from my job so I bought a pearl and gold heart pin at the Beverly Wilshire gift shop. I paid $20.00 for the costume jewelry and you were very upset with me when I showed it to you. You said, 'It is very beautiful Pat but you paid too much for it! If I can find that very same pin for less money will you take it back?' Of course you found the very same pin for just $1.00 in a thrift store, you were amazing!"

"Mom, you are a real dynamic woman, a genuine fighter and against all odds you made it to 100 years of age!"

"I love you and hope you have a very happy birthday with many more celebrations for the years ahead!"

Your daughter, Pat
(Pat passed away in 2005 of cancer.

CHAPTER 21

ASSISTED LIVING FACILITY

Mom never seemed satisfied with her assisted living accommodations and I ended up moving her seven times from one place to another, until she finally settled on one that she liked in Margate, Florida. During one move, the moving company stole all her furniture and insisted that if they gave it back she would have to pay three times the moving quote. After the police arrested the owners, I got half of Mom's belongings back. That was quite an experience!

From the ages of 96 to 102 ½ Mom lived her life at the many assisted living facilities. She always made it know that it was difficult living with the "old folks" who can't hear, are not lucid, and are always falling asleep during a conversation. It took some time before Mom accepted her living arrangements, but she persevered, and it didn't take her long before she got herself around the facility, pushing her four-wheeled walker from one activity to another.

Mom still had all her marbles and at 100 years old, she was still sharp as a tack! Her favorite games were Bingo and Rummikub. When she tried to play Bridge the players fell asleep so she had to give up the game. She loved to get dressed up and attended every party at the ALF. When Saturday came around, that was the day she went shopping at the local flea market. She also traveled in the facility's van with the group to movies, shows, and of course special dinners at the local restaurants. Mom still had a good appetite and could devour a good meal with no problem!

Because she was one of the oldest residents at the ALF, she was chosen to speak to a newspaper reporter who was doing a story about Centenarians. Mom was very excited and called me to be part of this interview. We had our pictures taken together and we were featured in the television newscast. It was very exciting!

Assisted Living Facility

Newspaper Article 2003

MINNIE WARSCHAUER, 101
ANNE DOBKIN, 57

The centenarian: Minnie Warschauer of Margate had two older brothers die of heart disease in their 70s; another died at 86. But her 89-year-old sister still is living, having made it through heart surgery. When she was young, Warschauer survived a serious automobile accident and an emergency Caesarian section. Within the past several years, she also has fully recovered from a mastectomy after she was diagnosed with breast cancer, and a broken leg. Today, she is one of three centenarians living in her Margate nursing home, and she exercises every day. "They call me Wonder Woman," Warschauer says.

The child: Anne Dobkin of Deerfield Beach, a medical assistant and birthing coach, was her mother's last child, born when Warschauer was 44. Her father died of a heart attack when he was 45 but Dobkin's older sisters, both in their mid-70s, still are living. "The women in our family live a long time, and we don't look our chronological age," she says.

How they are similar: Mother and daughter battle high cholesterol yet have low blood pressure. Dobkin says they both also are strong-willed, independent women who aren't afraid of challenges.

How they are different: Dobkin picked up her mother's dedication to exercise, eating right and maintaining her appearance — but not quite to the same extreme. "My mother grew our food in our back yard when I was growing up because she didn't want to eat anything processed," Dobkin says. Warschauer also refuses any medicines or treatments she doesn't think she needs.

Mom continued to be active and was looking forward to her 102nd birthday party at the ALF. Being the oldest resident she was given a big celebration, with ice cream and cake, balloons and presents.

The last six months of her life she seemed to lose interest in her daily activities. She was in bed a lot and had a hospice nurse with her. She told me "it was time to go to heaven", but I told her "she had to be called first". The nurse was confused when Mom kept calling out her phone number. The nurse chuckled when I told her "Mom wanted to be called to heaven".

There were times when Mom would not get out of bed or eat anything. She grew weaker by the day. It was a few days before Thanksgiving when Mom got herself out of bed and dressed with the help of the nurse's aide. She asked to go to breakfast and was wheeled down to the dining room. She ate a small amount but seemed too weak to finish it. She then asked to be taken back to her room to lie down. Awhile later the nurse came to check on her and found no pulse or blood pressure. Mom had a smile on her face and a pink glow on her checks. She had passed away peacefully, just as she had planned. She always said, "When I go to heaven I want to go in my sleep." Her last wish was granted!

Mom was quit a lady who knew exactly how she wanted to live, laugh and love life, doing it her way to the end of her dying day!

PART THREE

Secrets to A Long Life

"Think positive, eat healthy and have fun all the way to 101!"

CHAPTER 22

YOU ARE WHAT YOU EAT

Mom believed in cleansing out the body to get rid of toxins and stay healthy within. She would fast once a week, drink fresh squeezed, hot lemon water and flush out her system with an enema. She also believed in natural laxatives like 'Milk of Magnesia' or a dried grass called 'Swiss Kriss'.

Her eating habits were unconventional for that era. She ate only fresh, organic foods and drank pure water from the health food store. Her backyard had many fruit trees. Each day she would go outside and pick fresh avocados, oranges, lemons, apples and peaches to eat.

If she felt sick, which was rare, she would make a concoction of hot tea with organic, raw honey and a fresh squeezed lemon, and she would drink it every hour with a 100 mg Vitamin C pill. For any congestion she believed in 'Vicks Vapor Rub', which she applied to the chest and under the nose every night to open up the nasal air passages and sinuses. With her natural treatments and positive thinking that she was going to rid her body of the virus, it was good-bye cold!

She only ate brown foods consisting of whole wheat, pumpernickel or rye breads, brown rice, brown sugar, brown whole wheat flour for baking, and brown cereal. Except for occasional cornmeal mush or Cream of Wheat, she stuck to that diet.

Mom's daily meals consisted of either a fresh picked avocado with cottage cheese, fresh green salad, organic vanilla yogurt with fresh fruit, or a soup concoction I called the "pot on the stove". This special large pot contained fresh cut up vegetables, a fresh cut up chicken with the bones, and special seasonings simmered to perfection. She made enough for a week's worth of meals and then drank what was left. She called it the "vitamin soup".

She stayed away from frozen, processed or any foods that were not freshly made. Her daily breakfast consisted of freshly squeezed orange juice from oranges in her yard. A 3-minute egg, rye toast spread with butter and homemade jam, as well as a freshly brewed cup of coffee. She sprinkled brewer's yeast over her dark brown cereal as it was a potent powder for vitality and energy. When in season, she ate a half of a fresh melon or grapefruit. After she boiled her egg, she drank the egg water because she knew it had calcium from the shells. The eggshells went into her rose garden along with the coffee grinds. Her roses were magnificent, with vivid colors of pink, yellow, peach and red.

Occasionally, Mom did enjoy special treats like cracking the shells of mixed nuts and eating a handful. She also loved a few pieces of 'Seas Candy' that consisted of dark chocolate with nuts. But her very favorite treat was a slice of warm, homemade Granny Smith apple pie with vanilla ice cream. She did have a sweet tooth and was slightly overweight with a pear shaped figure.

She took supplements from the health food store along with hot lemon water and Vitamin C to keep her immune system healthy and strong. She knew that the body needed to be in an alkaline state for the immune system to fight off any illness or infections. She was way ahead of her time with nutritional knowledge and knew that the only thing that could override a healthy immune system was acidity and stress.

Mom believed in a 95 percent organic plant based diet with some fresh fish, turkey or chicken which she added to her pot on the stove. She would chew her food slowly and eat less by choosing a smaller plate size and stopping before she felt full. Her main meal was at lunch and a smaller meal at night. She enjoyed one glass of red wine a day, possibly boosting her longevity.

Mom had a very large, mature avocado tree which bore her fresh fruit year around. She would pick one each day, cut it in half and put fresh lemon juice on it. She also enjoyed eating them in her salads. She knew that avocados had a lot of healthy nutrients.

Mom had a fig tree that bore sweet, succulent fruit. She claimed figs were good to relieve constipation, as they are high in fiber and just a few would do. We both picked the delicious fruit when ripe and before the birds devoured them. Mom knew that figs are a powerhouse of nutrients and are highly alkaline, which can keep the body out of the acid zone.

Mom also had a lemon tree and picked at least a dozen lemons a week. She was adamant about her daily mug of lemon water each morning. I had a saying, "Mom stayed in the pink with her lemon drink"! She had a saying, "A lemon a day keeps the doctor away"! She knew lemons are loaded with vitamin C that helps to boost the immune system. They are acidic fruit before eaten but when consumed and metabolized by the body, lemons become alkaline. If you want to drink lemon juice always dilute the juice of one lemon with an 8 oz. glass of water and some liquid Stevia or raw honey to sweeten. Sparkling mineral water makes it taste like a healthy lemonade soda. Be sure to sip from a straw if you are prone to tooth sensitivity.

Mom loved using raw, organic honey in her lemon drink, on her cereal, or in hot tea. She would buy it fresh from the health food store because the honey was pure and full of nutrients. When she had a cold or sore throat she would make hot tea with lemon and honey and drink it every hour until she felt better.

INTERESTING FACTS ABOUT SOME OF MOM'S FAVORITE FOODS*

CARROTS: A large sliced carrot looks like a human eye and are known for eye health.

TOMATOES: A sliced tomato has four chambers, are red like the heart and are good for the heart and blood system.

WALNUTS: Walnuts look like a brain and are known to help brain functions.

ONIONS: Onions look like the cells of the body and help clear waste material from our cells.

CELERY: Celery resemble bones and contribute to bone strength due to their 23% sodium content which is the same as bones.

FIGS: Figs resemble testicles, are full of seeds, and hang as pairs as they grow. They might help with fertility.

AVOCADOS: Avocados are shaped like a uterus and like a full term baby, the fruit takes nine months to grow from bloom to ripened fruit.

CITRUS FRUIT: Kiwi, lemons and limes resemble the inside of mammary glands and might assist in breast health.

*Sources David Bjerklie, TIME Magazine, 2003 and Wikipedia

CHAPTER 23

YOU ARE WHAT YOU THINK

Mom always had a happy demeanor. Instead of feeling down and depressed she would turn the problem around and find an answer.

It is said, " that people who are happy and have a positive outlook on life tend to live longer than people who feel down and depressed. Happier people can have a lower risk of heart disease, stroke, cancer, diabetes and disabilities. A positive attitude helps to slow the heart rate, lowers blood pressure and improves sleep."

"Unhappy people, who have a negative outlook on life, produce the stress hormone cortisol. When you are stressed most likely you reach for sugar foods and high carb snacks that can cause you to eat more and gain weight."

Mom loved comedy shows on television and had a belly laugh each day. She felt a good laugh exercised the internal organs. She also surrounded herself with like-minded people who shared good news and also loved to laugh. She knew that in order to transform her mind to feeling good she had to have control of her thoughts.

She knew that trusting life would bring exactly what she needed. To worry about problems only created stress and anxiety. She would take a problem and work towards a positive outcome instead of getting overwhelmed and exhausted.

She always persevered, no matter what got in her way! That is how Mom lived her last 50 years of her life. Her most important longevity secrets were positive thinking, eating healthy, organic foods and having fun all the way to 101!

"A positive attitude causes a chain reaction of positive thoughts, events, and outcomes. It is a catalyst and it sparks extraordinary results."

Wade Boggs

~

"Loving yourself makes you feel good, and good health comes from feeling good."

Louise Hay

~

Someone asked us recently...
"Is there any limitation to the body's ability to heal?"
And we said, "None, other than the belief that you hold."

Abraham

CHAPTER 24

THE SECRETS TO LONGEVITY

Studying *The Law of Attraction* could help you to change your thoughts to more positive ones. Every daydream can be turned into a reality. You are what you think and will attract that vibration, so try and bring up your vibration to a happier level of thought and see wonderful changes in your life!

Newborn babies can be born with a negative demeanor and cry and fuss a lot. Some newborns just look around and are content, only to cry to get attention when it is feeding time or to have their diaper changed. But, as they grow up, each has a choice to be happy or not.

Spend time in nature and look at the beauty that surrounds you. Go outside and observe the birds, clouds, trees, sunsets or sunrises, and work in your garden planting flowers. Doing these activities can change your attitude to a more positive outlook. Try planting a butterfly garden and watch beautiful butterflies visit your garden. It will improve your mood, spark creativity and lower your anxiety levels.

Laughter is also good for the body and soul. It stimulates the organs and releases stress. See a comedy movie, read a funny book or just play with your cat or dog which should bring a smile to your face and make you very happy.

Keep a gratitude journal and write down your blessings you have each day. Try and reframe your perception from negative to positive thoughts about life, work, family, relationships or whatever situation you find yourself in at that moment. Stay away from negative people who bring your good vibrations down.

Meditate, listen to your favorite music, have a massage, hug and kiss your lover each day or just pray for peace in your life and the world. These activities will support emotional freedom and happiness.

Social Connections*

Stronger social connections with friends and family and a faith based community can add years to your life. Also, living near or 'Skyping' your extended family by connecting with children, grandchildren, and parents during holidays and special occasions can possibly give you a longer life expectancy. Having a loving, caring life partner can be positive as well. Join clubs or take classes of interest to keep your brain cells active.

Have a Life Purpose*

A buffer against mortality is to have an activity, passion or work that motivates you and gives you a purpose to get up in the morning. Joining an interest group like ballroom dancing, painting, bike riding, volunteering or whatever you desire to do, can contribute to longevity.

Get Physical*

Keeping in shape in the golden years adds years to your life and keeps your bones stronger. If you love to garden, bike ride, walk, play golf or tennis, do yoga and other sorts of pleasurable activities, exercising can be fun! If you enjoy working out in a gym, that can also be a good, structured exercise to keep your body strong.

*"It's True: Optimists Live Longer than Pessimists." By James E. Lemire, M.D.
**Parade Magazine, April 5, 2015, "Cheater's Guide to Living to 100". By Dan Buettner.

CHAPTER 25

A SUMMARY OF MOM'S LONGEVITY SECRETS

Mom lived by the following daily regiments which kept her on track to reach her goal of becoming a Centenarian:

Feisty, independent and strong willed.

She was not afraid to state her case and continued to solve any unsettling situations until she was satisfied with the results.

She was not intimidated by anything or anyone.

She only ate natural, organic home grown foods and grew most of her fruits and vegetables in her backyard. She never ate canned, frozen, or processed foods. She only ate brown bread, cereal, and rice. She used brown flour and brown sugar for baking.

She detoxed her system once a week by drinking hot lemon water all day, as well as taking an enema and a laxative.

She would visit a health spa to drink natural mineral water from an underground spring and enjoyed the mud baths, salt massages and nude sun baths.

Her exercise regiments consisted of yoga, *Jack La Lane* television program, ballroom dancing and gardening.

She rested on a slant board each day with slices of cucumbers on her eyes to reduce under eye puffiness.

She took a daily nap before going out for the evening.

She liked to tell jokes and laugh out loud.

To keep her system healthy, she took supplements of vitamins and minerals which she bought at the health food store. She saw a doctor only in emergency situations.

She had cataracts later in life and had crystal lenses put into her eyes so that she did not need to wear glasses. Her hearing was good and in her last years it seemed she only would hear what she wanted to hear.

CHAPTER 26

MOM'S TEACHERS

EMMET FOX was a new thought minister, author, healer, scientist, philosopher and spiritual teacher who lived from 1886-1951. He encouraged people to develop their own creative power and personal understanding of what 'God' is all about. The theme of his teachings is, "Life is consciousness and we are what we think. Thoughts are things and all potential lies in their creative and constructive use". *

Mom read all his books and practiced putting his inspirations into her daily life. I feel that he had influenced her greatly, being her guide and teacher, getting her through her many adversities, and helping her bounce back to a more positive path throughout her life. She was not a religious woman but she had a great connection to the God Source and spirituality.

*Emmet Fox. *Power Through Constructive Thinking.*

GAYLORD HAUSER was an American nutritionist and self-help author. He promoted the 'natural way of eating' during the mid-20th century and is regarded as the founder of the natural food movement and a pioneer who was decades ahead of his time. He promoted foods rich in vitamin B and discouraged consumption of sugar and white flour.

He was born on May 17th, 1895 in Tubingen, Germany and sailed to America as a steerage passenger on the SS George Washington on August 14, 1911. After a serious illness, he recovered and studied 'food science' in order to become an expert and spread a message about the healing power of food.*

Mom read Hauser's books and followed the value of his five "wonder foods": yogurt, brewers yeast, powered skim milk, wheat germ, and blackstrap molasses.

She also followed what he had to say about healthful effects of "whole foods", avoided fats, excessive sugar, excessive consumption of meat, white bread, white flour, white sugar and white rice.

*Wikipedia, the free encyclopedia

CHAPTER 27

THE SCIENCE OF LONGEVITY

*THE LONGEVITY GENE #4

Scientists have pondered what enables centenarians to maintain good health for a long period of time. They think that centenarians have a history of aging very slowly and either delay age-related diseases such as heart problems, stroke, diabetes, cancer and Alzheimer's disease or avoid these health problems altogether. Centenarians lived long, not by surviving these diseases but by most likely avoiding them altogether. They also found that the centenarians have long–lived siblings and suspected genetics played a larger role than environment due to exceptionally old siblings.*

In Boston, MA, August 27, 2001 Researchers at Beth Israel Deaconess Medical Center, Children's Hospital and other institutions have found a region on human Chromosome #4 that is likely to contain a gene or genes associated with and play a role in extraordinary life expectancy

CHAPTER 28

TELOMERES

Telomeres are part of the cell DNA and have a distinct purpose involved with the process of cell division. Each time a cell divides the telomeres on the ends of the chromosome shorten until eventually cell division and replication come to a halt and a person dies.*

There is a substance called telomerase, which can maintain or lengthen the telomere and in turn may play a role in how a person ages quickly or slowly. Some scientists believe that the gene for telomerase may play a pivotal role in how quickly or slowly cells, and people, age. Telomere shortening does play an important role in aging faster.*

People who age slowly look much younger than what is expected for their ages. A woman who has a child late in life and/or goes through menopause in her late 50's, like Mom, might possible have longer telomeres. Her doctors always told her "that her body functions were at least 10 years younger than her age". Her mind, sight and hearing were still very good at 100 years of age.

Living to 100 by Thomas T. Perls, MD., M.P. and Margery Hunter Silver, Ed.D with John F. Lauerman pages 122-123

EPILOGUE

Finishing Mom's biography, I not only feel a sense of great accomplishment for making her life wish come true, but also that I finally gave birth to her long awaited book. The outline sat on the shelf for many years and awaken when I got the desire to write and complete my first endeavor with book writing. Even though I wrote a full length screenplay, book writing was another genre to learn.

Recently, I went to a medium because my little dachshund, Muffie, had just died and I was hoping she might come through with a message. But to my surprise, Mom came through first. The medium said that Mom would not let anyone else talk and believe me she had a lot to say, as usual! The most astonishing statement that my mother made was, "Anne, I am very proud of you. You finally finished my book and I know it will be a success. It should help thousands of people change their lives and I will be smiling when that happens."

I could not believe the medium conveyed that message to me as I did not tell her anything about Mom or the book I was writing. She also said, "she has a dog here and this dog thanks Mollee for taking good care of her." I never told the medium about my two dachshunds, Mollee and Muffie.

Because I had a good reading by this wonderful medium, I truly believe that our loved ones and friends live on and are always with us. When I write I am very surprised that the words flow through me and onto the computer keys. There is no doubt in my mind that Mom and Dad are guiding me not only in my writing but also throughout my life.

As Mom would often say:

LIVE FOR TODAY

LAUGH OFTEN

LOVE ALWAYS

ABOUT THE AUTHOR

Anne Dobkin

Anne grew up in Westwood, California and attended UCLA. She studied to be a nurse and worked privately in postpartum homecare. Needing more excitement Anne switched to a career in the stock brokerage and real estate investment/sales business. Retiring at the age of 53, she went back to work part time in postpartum homecare and also became certified as a birthing coach/doula.

At 25 years of age she married and moved to New Jersey where her two children were born. She divorced after 17 years of marriage and moved to Boca Raton, Florida where she enjoyed the beach, golf and played team tennis.

Anne began her writing career 15 years ago. Her first project was a screenplay, based on a true story about a camping trip her family took in a 20 foot, dilapidated old RV camper, to the Great Smokey Mountains of Tennessee. Unfortunately, due to a comedy of errors, they did not get passed Virginia Beach, Virginia.

The trip turned into such a disaster that she was inspired to write a screenplay and enter it into a screenwriter's competition. Even though the true story never made it to Hollywood, Anne plans on recreating the screenplay into a very funny novel.

As mostly a satire writer, Anne can see comedy in almost all of life's situations. Even when there are dire circumstances, she can find something funny to inspire her to create a story from it.

About the Author

Anne lives in The Villages, Florida where there are many opportunities to learn book writing and self-publishing. She is grateful for these informative courses to help make her dream of becoming an authentic author come true. She has three more books in the works and she will be very busy writing for at least the next five years!

Anne plays pickleball, golf, Mahjongg, and visits her two children and five grandchildren in New Jersey and South Florida. She lives with her adorable, long hair mini dachshund named Mollee and enjoys dancing, playing golf and traveling with her significant other.

Made in the USA
Charleston, SC
19 December 2015